Play Piano Today!

by Amy Appleby
With this proven play-as-you-learn method,
you can master the basics of playing the piano in just a few weeks!

Cover photograph by Randall Wallace

This book Copyright © 2001 by Amsco Publications,
A Division of Music Sales Corporation, New York

Order No. AM 971355
US International Standard Book Number: 0.8256.1894.0
UK International Standard Book Number: 0.7119.8972.9

Exclusive Distributors:
Music Sales Corporation
257 Park Avenue South, New York, NY 10010 USA
Music Sales Limited
8/9 Frith Street, London W1D 3JB England
Music Sales Pty. Limited
120 Rothschild Street, Rosebery, Sydney, NSW 2018, Australia

Printed in the United States of America by
Vicks Lithograph and Printing Corporation

Amsco Publications
New York/London/Paris/Sydney/Copenhagen/Madrid

Compact Disc Track Listing

Contents

Introduction

This interactive piano course will guide you through the basics of piano performance and technique. As you learn to play a wide range of piano solos, you'll explore the essentials of music theory and learn how to read music in standard notation. You'll find that your playing skills will develop quickly as you practice and perform using the backup tracks provided on the accompanying CD.

This proven method has helped thousands of piano students to perform music in a wide range of styles. Here you will find the very best of blues, rock, pop, folk, ragtime, jazz, and classical music in rewarding piano arrangements. Popular selections include chart-toppers by Elvis Presley, the Beach Boys, the Animals—as well as hits by James Taylor, Judy Collins, Bing Crosby, and Ella Fitzgerald. Here you will also find the all-time favorite songs that every pianist needs to know for performing at special occasions and parties—such as "The Entertainer," "For He's a Jolly Good Fellow," "Bridal Chorus," and "Jingle Bells."

At the end of this course, you will be able to play dozens of great songs on the piano. You will also be able to sightread piano music in different keys—and you'll have the skills you need to learn hundreds of new songs on your own.

Your Piano

This book is designed to be used with any keyboard instrument—ranging from a medium-sized electric piano to a concert grand. If you are using an electronic keyboard, it should have at least twenty-nine white keys (or forty-nine total keys). If it's a tabletop electronic piano or synthesizer, be sure the instrument is on a table that allows enough room for your knees and thighs when you sit in front of it on a sturdy bench or straight-backed, armless chair. (Should your electronic keyboard be mounted on an adjustable stand, you may want to reposition it to a comfortable height.)

If you are using a non-electric (or acoustic) piano, you must be sure your instrument is in tune before you begin to play. If the instrument has not been tuned in several months, chances are that you will need the services of a professional tuner. If you are using an electric piano or synthesizer, you can easily tune the instrument by adjusting the instruments master tuning control (refer to the manual for your instrument for detailed tuning instructions).

Turn on your CD player now and begin listening to the audio instruction for this course.

Notes on the Keyboard

Musical notes are named using the first seven letters of the alphabet. These letter names indicate notes in an ascending sequence—from low to high. After the final G note, the sequence begins again. A full-sized piano is able to repeat this pattern many times.

A—B—C—D—E—F—G, A—B—C—D—E—F—G, and so on.

The *black notes* of the piano occur in groups of two and three. The white key that occurs before every group of two black notes is a *C note.* The note labeled *Middle C* is the C note nearest to the center of the keyboard.

Middle C

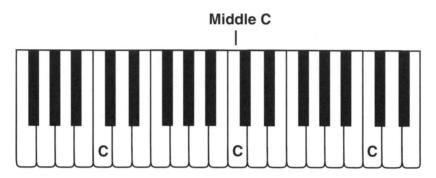

Get into a comfortable playing position in front of the piano, find Middle C and play it once. Now, beginning at the lowest C note on your keyboard, find and play every C note in sequence, from lowest to highest. Notice that, although each new C note is obviously higher than the next, they all sound like different versions of the same note.

The white key that occurs before every group of three black notes is an *F note.* Play every F note on the keyboard, from lowest to highest.

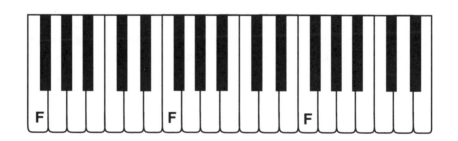

As you can see, the black-note groupings provide the pianist with a frame of reference for locating and playing the white keys on the piano keyboard. In the keyboard diagram that follows, a *D note* occurs in the middle of every group of two black keys, and *E note* occurs immediately after every group of two black keys, and so on. Take the time to memorize the letter names of the white keys of the piano keyboard.

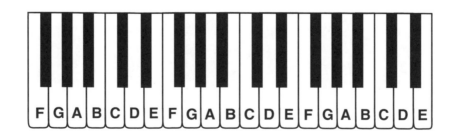

The Right Hand

The pianist frequently plays in the *middle range* of the keyboard. Let's take a look at some of the keys in this range.

Place your right thumb on Middle C (as indicated by the finger number **1**). Place the fingers of your right hand (**2, 3, 4,** and **5**) on consecutive white keys, as shown. This hand position is called *C Position*. Play these notes in sequence now.

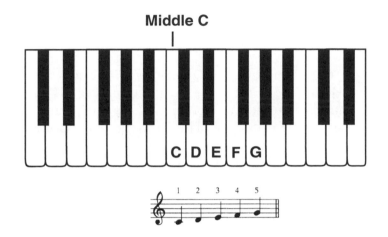

Now play the same sequence backward, beginning with the right pinky (**5**) on the G note.

Next play these two sequences together, beginning with the thumb (**1**).

Take the time to practice the above exercise until you can play it evenly and smoothly.
Here are some things to remember as you play.

- Keep your fingers curved and relaxed.

- Depress each key fully and firmly with the fingertip.

- Lift each finger just as the next finger goes down (so each note has the same time value).

Notes on the Staff

Written music is a universal language of notes and symbols. These are arranged on the musical *staff,* which consists of five lines and four spaces. Let's take another look at the five notes you have just played. The notes in this sequence advance by *steps* as they move through the alternating lines and spaces.

C D E F G

The sign at the beginning of this staff is known as a *treble clef.* This clef is also called the *G clef,* because it curls around the second line of the staff—the position of the G note. This note serves as a point of reference for naming all other notes on the staff. In most piano music, the treble clef is used to mark the part played by the right hand. This hand is often responsible for playing the tune (or *melody*) of a piece.

Rhythm Basics

Each note on the staff tells you which key (or *pitch*) to play on the keyboard, and how long the tone should last. The combined *note values* of a melody form its *rhythm.*

The basic unit of rhythm in music is called a *beat.* Musical notes range in length from just a fraction of a beat to a duration of several beats. Once you are familiar with note values and musical counting, you'll be able to sightread the melodies of hundreds of songs on your own.

Sometimes the term rhythm is used to describe the overall rhythmic "feel" or underlying "beat" of a song, as in "rock rhythm" or "Latin rhythm." You'll have the chance to explore these and other popular styles later on. The sections that follow focus on how notes are used to indicate rhythm in all types of written music. The best way to learn about rhythm is to play it. So get ready to play some great tunes as you master the basics of note values and musical time.

Basic Note Values

Familiarize yourself with the duration of these basic notes. The *quarter note* and *half note* feature a line or *stem.* The dot (or *notehead*) of the quarter note is solid, while the noteheads of the half note and *whole note* are outlined.

- ♩ Quarter Note = 1 beat

- ♩ Half Note = 2 beats

- o Whole Note = 4 beats

These basic note values form a pattern. The half note (which lasts for two beats) is twice the length of the quarter note (one beat). Similarly, the whole note (four beats) is twice the length of the half note (two beats).

Take a look at the first phrase of the traditional melody "Jingle Bells," which contains each of these note values.

⁴⁄₄ Time

One important key to the overall rhythm of a piece is the *time signature,* a numerical symbol that appears after the clef at the beginning of a piece of music. The time signature used in the following excerpt from "Jingle Bells" indicates that the piece is written in ⁴⁄₄ *time* (pronounced "four-four time").

The top number of this time signature (**4**) indicates that there are four beats per measure—and the bottom number (**4**) indicates that a quarter note gets one beat. The symbol **C** is also sometimes used to indicate ⁴⁄₄ time.

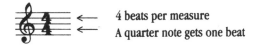

Barlines divide each *bar* (or *measure*) of the melody into four equal beats (counted "**1**-2-**3**-4," with a stress on the first and third beat of each measure). A *double barline* marks the end of the excerpt.

Count each beat aloud as you clap the rhythm of "Jingle Bells"—that is, count out each beat number slowly and evenly, but clap only on the beats that correspond to notes of the melody as indicated by the beat numbers that appear in boxes.

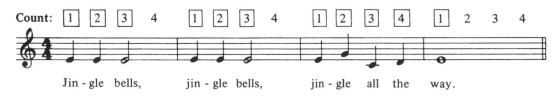

Now place your right hand in C Position (with the thumb on Middle C) and play this phrase of "Jingle Bells," beginning with the third finger on the E note. Count each beat as you play

Eighth Notes

Many tunes contain short notes that are worth only one-half of a beat. These notes are called *eighth notes.*

♪ **Eighth Note** = ½ beat

Eighth notes often occur in groups of two or more. Each group is linked with a bar or *beam.* Count the rhythm of this example aloud. Note that eighth notes are counted with the word "and" between beats in the second measure.

Now take a look at the rhythm in the second phrase of "Jingle Bells." Count each beat number aloud—and clap on the beats that appear in boxes to indicate each note of the melody.

Place your right hand in C Position and play the full chorus of "Jingle Bells," beginning with the third finger on the E note. Practice "Jingle Bells" (without counting) until you can play it smoothly and evenly. Next, set your book aside and try playing this song from memory.

Jingle Bells

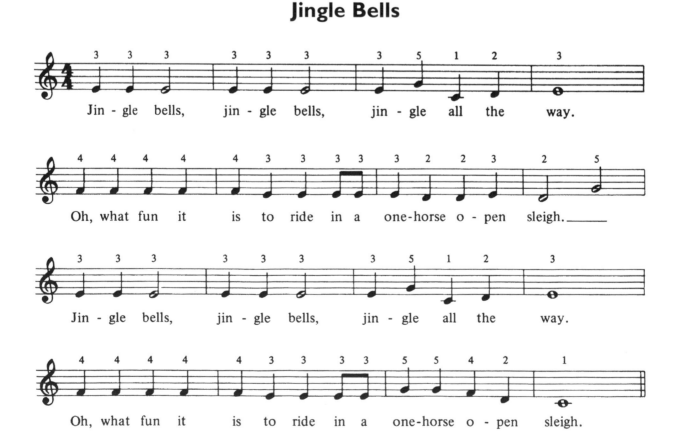

Sightreading a Melody

Reading music (or *sightreading*) is an important skill for any pianist. The best way to develop your sightreading ability is to learn new songs. At this point, you are ready to sightread any melody in C Position.

Position the thumb of your right hand on Middle C and play the theme of Beethoven's "Ode to Joy" slowly and evenly, beginning with the third finger on the E note.

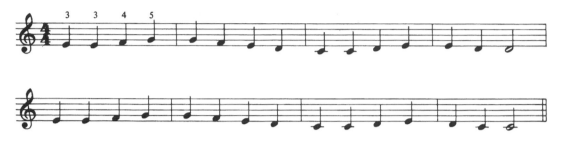

The Left Hand

In most piano music, the left hand is responsible for playing the accompaniment (or harmony) of a piece. The clef used to mark music for the left hand is called the *bass clef*. This clef is also known as the *F clef* because it curls around the fourth line up from the bottom of the staff and highlights that line with two dots. This marks the position of the F note, which serves as a point of reference for naming all other notes on the bass staff.

Place the pinky of your left hand on *Low C* (that's the C note below Middle C). Play these notes in sequence, beginning with the pinky (5) on Low C.

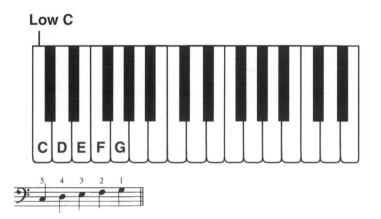

Now play the same sequence backward, beginning with the thumb (1) on the G note.

Now play these two sequences together, beginning with the pinky (5) on Low C.

Playing the Harmony

Most piano music is written on the *grand staff*, which is made up of the treble staff and the bass staff linked together by a *brace*.

Take a look at Beethoven's "Ode to Joy," as notated on the grand staff. The staff with the treble clef on top shows the melody, which is played by the right hand. The bass staff below shows music played by the left hand—the harmony.

Place your left hand in C Position—with the pinky (**5**) on the C note below Middle C. Now practice the left hand part of "Ode to Joy."

Remember, each whole note lasts for four beats. The half notes in the last measure each last for two beats. Count 1-2-3-4 evenly aloud as you play the left-hand part.

Once you are familiar with the left-hand part, try putting it together with the right-hand part.

Play this piece at a slow, even pace until you are quite familiar with it.

Ode to Joy

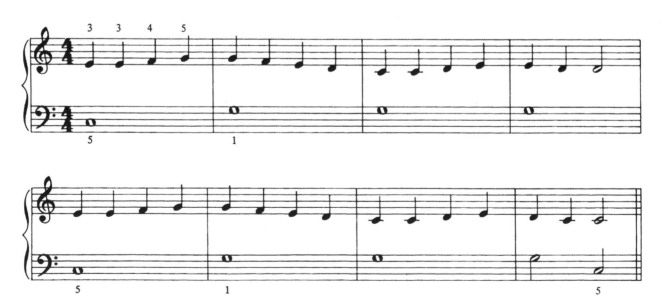

The C Major Scale

So far, you've practiced five tones—C, D, E, F, and G. Three more notes are needed to form the *C Major scale*—A, B, and the C note above Middle C.

Notice how the C major scale begins and ends on a C note—and contains eight tones. The distance between the two C notes is called an *octave*.

When you play this scale, cross your thumb under your third finger to play the F note. Practice playing this ascending C major scale until you can play it smoothly and evenly. Take the time to memorize the names and positions of the new notes in this scale.

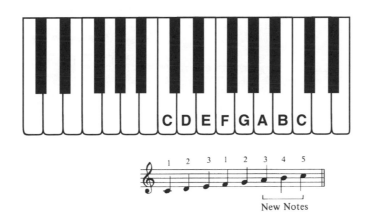

This is the C major scale in bass clef. Begin playing this scale with your left pinky on Low C. Remember to cross your third finger over your thumb to play the A note, as shown.

Practice playing the ascending C major scale with your left hand until you can play it smoothly and evenly.

Chord Basics

A *chord* is a group of three or more notes played together. A three-note chord is called a *triad*. Once you know how to play a few chords, you'll be able to figure out the harmony to many different songs on your own.

This section covers the basic chord forms that musicians use to read charts and create their own piano arrangements. First let's look at how the eight tones of the C major scale are used to form basic triads in the key of C major. Note that the eight triads are marked with Roman numerals—and that the last chord is actually just a higher version of the first. (You'll learn more about the individual qualities of these basic chords later on.)

Using the thumb, middle finger, and pinky of your right hand, play each of these chords in sequence up the scale, as shown. Note the finger numbers at the left of each chord.

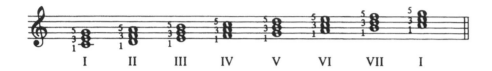

Now position your left pinky on Low C and play five chords with the left hand.

The two most important chords in any key are the *I chord* and *V chord* (pronounced "one chord" and "five chord"). As their names imply, these chords are built on the first and fifth degrees of the scale. In the key of C, the I and V chords are called the *C chord* and *G chord,* respectively, to correspond with the letter names of their lowest notes.

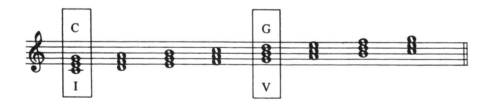

The lowest note of each of these triads is called the *root,* the middle note is called the *third,* and the top note is called the *fifth.* Normally, these tones are played by the pianist's first, third, and fifth fingers, respectively. Here are the C and G chords notated for the left hand in bass clef. Try playing these now.

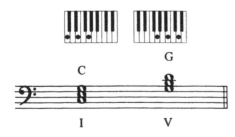

Chord Inversion

In order to make it easy to alternate between the C and G chords with the left hand, let's rearrange the notes of the C triad so that the fifth of the chord (or G note) is played as the bass note of the triad, as shown—and the first and third (C and E) are moved up one octave. When the notes of a triad are rearranged in this way, the chord is called an *inversion*.

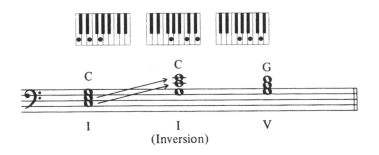

Practice these chords with the left hand until you can play them evenly and smoothly. Allow each chord to last for four beats.

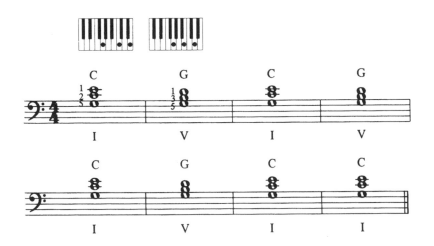

Now practice this exercise with the right hand, using an extended version of *G Position*. Notice that the B note is skipped—and your third, fourth, and fifth fingers must stretch up one key to play the pattern, which features a new note at the top—the E note.

Get ready to play the tune "Tom Dooley" with your right hand in G Position, beginning with your thumb (**1**) on the G note. This traditional American song was a number one hit for the Kingston Trio in 1958—and remained on the pop charts for eighteen weeks.

Note that the chord symbols C and G are shown above the staff to indicate the chords played by the left hand. The corresponding Roman numeral chord symbols, I and V, are listed below the staff.

Tom Dooley

The G7 Chord

If you add or change one or more notes of a triad, you create an *altered chord*. The V chord is often altered by adding the seventh tone above the root tone. The resulting chord is known as a *V7 chord* (pronounced "five-seven chord"). In the key of C, this chord is called the *G7 chord*. Here are the C and G7 chords in treble clef.

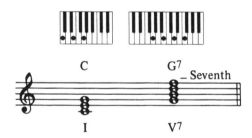

In order to make it easy to play the C and G7 chords in one position, the G7 chord should be rearranged to form this inversion. The third of the chord becomes the bass note, and the fifth of the chord is omitted.

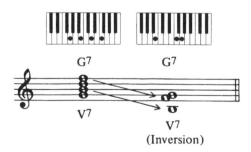

Here are the C and G7 chords in a bass clef exercise. Practice playing these chords with the left hand. Finger the V7 chord with your left pinky, index finger, and thumb (**5, 2,** and **1**). Hold each chord for four beats.

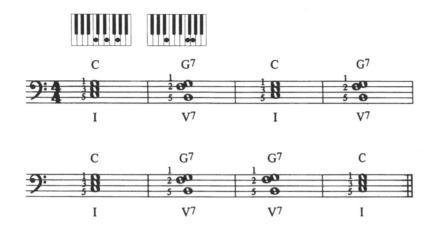

Once you can play this exercise smoothly, take a look at "Go Tell Aunt Rhody." Practice the melody first with your right hand. When you feel familiar with the melody, add the chords with the left hand.

Go Tell Aunt Rhody

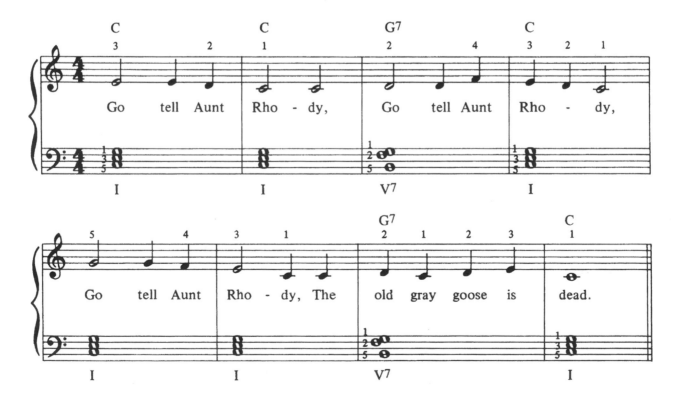

The F Chord

The *F chord* is built on the fourth note of the C scale and is called the *IV chord* in the key of C (pronounced "four chord"). Like the C and G chords, the F chord is made up of a root, third, and fifth.

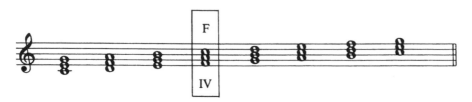

This inversion of the F chord (with the fifth of the triad moved to the lowest position) makes it convenient to play the F chord with the C and G7 chords.

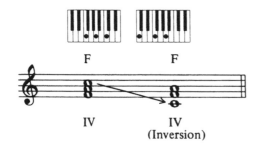

Here's the F chord in bass clef. Note the pinky plays the C note, while the index finger and thumb must stretch up to play the F and A notes, respectively.

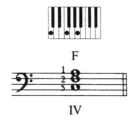

This chord exercise contains the C, G7, and F chords (the I, V7, and IV chords in the key of C). Practice the exercise with the left hand until you can play it evenly.

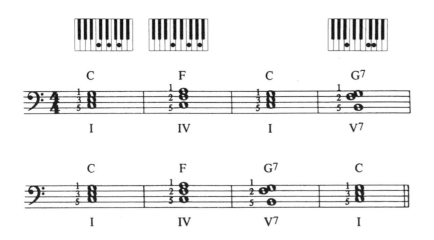

Now play "Jingle Bells" with both hands. (The right hand begins with the third finger on the E note.)

Jingle Bells

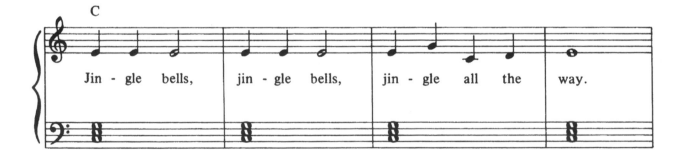

Rests

Most music is composed of sounds and silences. The silent beats in music are represented by signs called *rests*. Rests are named and valued in correspondence with the note values you learned previously.

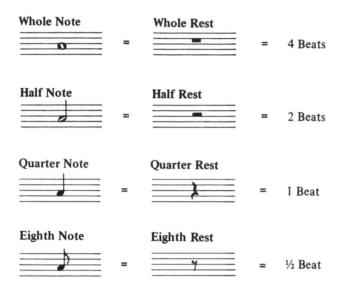

Rests and notes may be combined in the same measure, as long as their combined values add up to the correct number of beats (in this example, four beats to a measure). Count the beats of this phrase as you clap the rhythm of the notes.

Now play "Old MacDonald" with the right hand. Be sure to allow the appropriate number of silent beats where the rests occur in the melody. The fingering numbers will show you where you need to stretch your hand position to play melody notes.

Old MacDonald

Pickup Notes

A pickup is a note or notes that occur before the first stressed beat of the song. When a musical composition features a partial measure containing a pickup, it usually makes up the remaining beats of the first measure in the last measure of the piece. This means that the last measure of the piece will also be incomplete.

Count aloud as you play the melody of "Polly Wolly Doodle" with the right hand, beginning with the thumb on the C note. Once you are familiar with the right hand, play the piece with both hands together.

Polly Wolly Doodle

Ties and Slurs

A *tie* is a curved line that links two or more notes of the same pitch. This indicates that a tone be held for the combined length of the two tied notes. In this excerpt from "Careless Love," a tie links a whole note (four beats) and a half note (two beats). That means that the final C note should last for a total of six beats.

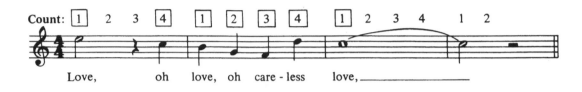

A *slur* is a curved line connecting two or more notes of different pitches. This mark indicates that the notes be played or sung in an smooth and connected manner called *legato*. In this excerpt from Edward Elgar's "Pomp and Circumstance" slurs are used to indicate legato playing.

A slur is always necessary in a song melody when two or more notes share one syllable of lyric, as shown in this passage from "Dixie."

Because of their similar appearance, ties are often confused with slurs. The way to tell them apart is to remember that ties link notes of the same pitch, while slurs always link notes of varying pitch.

This arrangement of "The Banks of the Ohio" features ties and slurs. Practice the right hand part until you can play it with ease. Remember, some slurs are necessary only because of a shared syllable in the lyric—and require no special attention on the part of the pianist. This type of slur occurs in "The Banks of the Ohio" at the words "a" and "flow."

Any additional slurs direct you to play the indicated notes legato. Such a slur occurs in the left hand in the last measure. Here the C chord should be smoothly played note by note.

The Banks of the Ohio

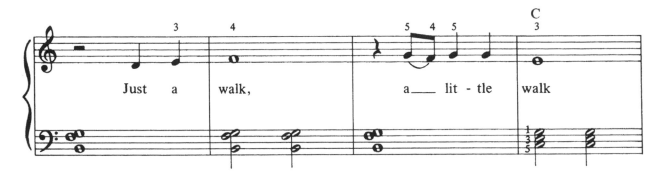

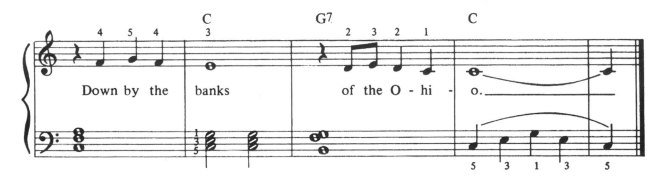

Repeats, Introductions, and Endings

Most styles of music call for their individual sections to be repeated at times. Two dots before a double bar from a repeat sign. If this sign occurs at the end of the piece, it indicates that you should repeat the entire piece once from the beginning. Play "Hot Cross Buns" twice through in tempo.

If a repeat sign occurs in the middle of a piece, go back to the beginning and repeat the section before going on.

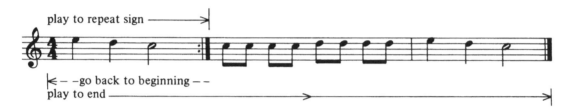

If a mirror image of the repeat sign occurs earlier in the piece, the performer should only repeat from that point onward. This version of "Hot Cross Buns" has a pickup measure at the beginning. The inverted repeat sign indicates that you should skip this measure when you repeat the piece.

Many song arrangements feature added music at the beginning of a piece called an *introduction* (or *intro*). Other arrangements feature added music to be played after the final verse of a piece (an *ending*). This version of "Hot Cross Buns" features an intro—as well as a first and second ending. The introduction and the first ending are played the first time through the piece. The second ending is played when the piece is repeated.

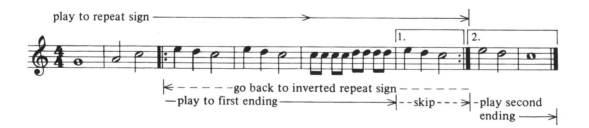

Now play "Kumbaya," which features an introduction and second ending. The first ending is played at the end of the first verse, while the second ending is played at the end of the second and final verse.

Kumbaya

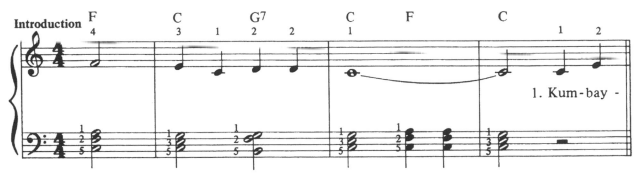

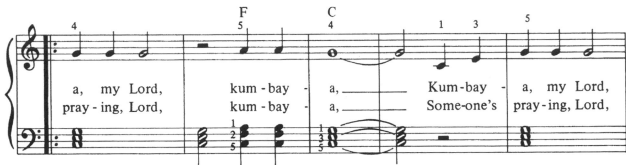

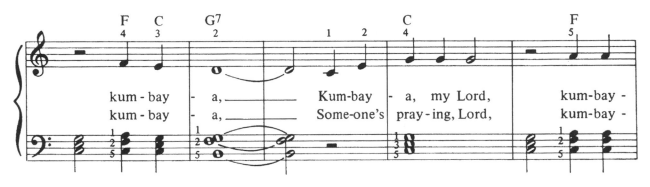

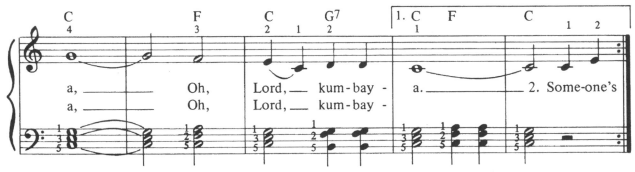

Dotted Notes and Rests

A dot placed after any note means that it should last one-and-a-half times its normal duration. For example, if you add a dot after a half note (which normally lasts two beats), you get a dotted half note, which lasts for three beats.

In the same way, when a dot is placed after a quarter note (which normally lasts one beat), a dotted quarter note results—which lasts for one-and-a-half beats. In the same way a dotted quarter rest lasts for one-and-a-half beats.

It's easy to understand dotted notes and rests when you compare them with the regular note and rest values you have already learned.

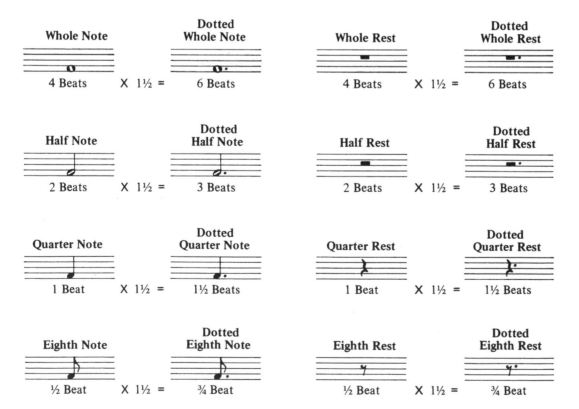

Take the time to memorize the appearance and value of each dotted note and rest. Then count and clap the first line of "Oh, Susanna"—an all-time favorite by Stephen Foster, which James Taylor revived on his album *Sweet Baby James.*

Notice that the dotted quarter and eighth note is a repeating pattern in the melody line and a dotted half note occurs at the end of each phrase of the song. Practice the right-hand part of this piece. Then play "Oh, Susanna" using both hands.

Oh, Susanna

¾ Time

Each of the songs you have played so far has been in ⁴₄ time—that is, with four beats to the measure. This metre is indicated by a time signature at the beginning of the piece.

Many songs are written in ¾ *time* ("three-four time") with three beats to a measure. This metre is also called *waltz time.* Take a look at the time signature for this popular metre.

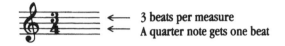
← 3 beats per measure
← A quarter note gets one beat

Get ready now to play "Drink to Me Only with Thine Eyes," as you count the indicated beats aloud ("**1**-2-3, **1**-2-3," and so on—with a stress on the first beat of every measure).

Notice that when two dotted half notes are tied together (as occurs in the last measure of this song) the total note value is six beats.

Also note that in ¾ time, the whole rest has a duration of three beats (not four beats, as in ⁴₄ time).

Remember that a whole rest lasts for the whole measure, regardless of the time signature.

Drink to Me Only with Thine Eyes

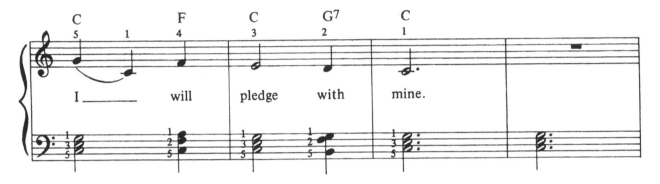

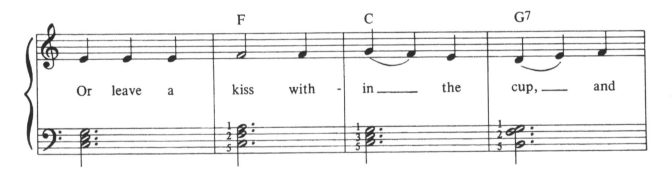

Broken Chords

You can add movement and power to a song by using *broken chords* in the harmony part. In this example, the bass tone of each chord is separated from the upper tones of the chord. With the left hand, practice this pattern of broken chords until you can play it smoothly.

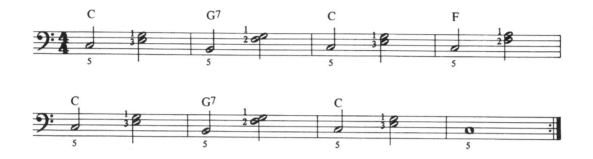

Now play "When the Saints Go Marching In." This familiar American spiritual was a popular hit for Bill Haley, who gave it a rock beat and retitled it "The Saints Rock 'n Roll."

Here, broken chords give this tune a distinctive rhythm. Notice that the last measure only has one beat—so, when you repeat the song, it forms a complete measure with the three-beat pick-up at the beginning.

When the Saints Go Marching In

Oh, when the saints go march-ing in, Oh, when the

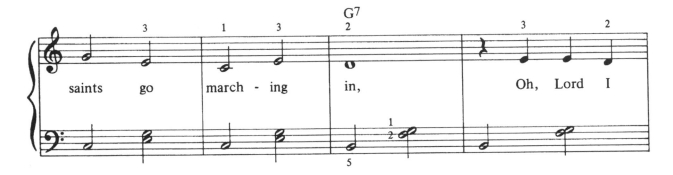

saints go march - ing in, Oh, Lord I

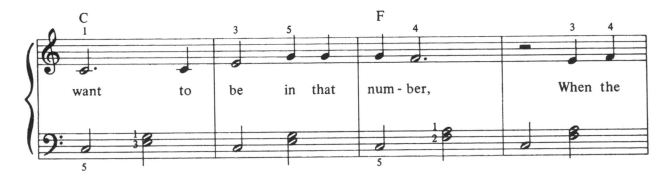

want to be in that num - ber, When the

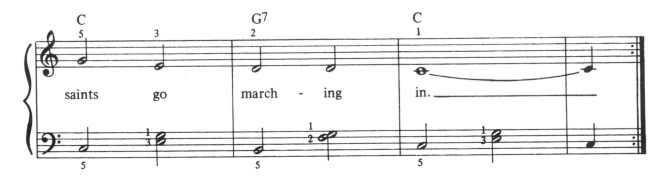

saints go march - ing in.

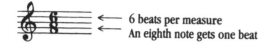 Time

Some time signatures call for the eighth note to last for one beat (instead of the usual quarter-note beat). Take a look at the time signature for ⁶⁄₈ *time.*

                    ⟵ 6 beats per measure
                    ⟵ An eighth note gets one beat

There are six beats in a measure, with an eighth note valued at one beat. In ⁶⁄₈ time, a stressed beat occurs every three eighth-note beats, providing two stresses in every measure. This is illustrated by boldface numbers in the first phrase of "The Irish Washerwoman." (As you can see, ⁶⁄₈ time has much of the same rhythmic feeling as ³⁄₄ time, with a stress on every third beat.)

5 6   1 2 3 4 5 6   1 2 3 4 5 6   1 2 3 4 5 6   1 2 3 4 5 6

Now combine your knowledge of ⁶⁄₈ time and dotted notes as you play "For He's a Jolly Good Fellow."

For He's a Jolly Good Fellow

Triplets

Composers and arrangers sometimes need to divide a basic note value into three notes of equal value. These three notes are collectively called a *triplet,* which is indicated by the numeral *3* above the notes. A quarter-note triplet normally lasts for two beats—and is indicated with a numeral *3* within a bracket. (Each note in this triplet is worth two-thirds of a beat.)

An eighth-note triplet normally lasts one beat—and is noted with a numeral *3* above the beam that links the three notes together. (Each note in this triplet is worth one-third of a beat.)

Triplets add a certain stately beauty to the powerful hymn "Amazing Grace." Clap and count the first line of this song using the words "three-and-ah" to correspond with the triplet in the first measure.

As a tribute to the lasting popularity of this song, Judy Collins made it a top-40 hit in 1971. The following year, the Royal Scots Dragoon Guards of Scotland's Armored Regiment recorded a bagpipe band version of this tune that put it back on the pop charts.

Practice the right-hand part before adding the chords with the left hand. The fingering numbers indicate where you should stretch or reposition your fingers. Play this one at a slow tempo.

Amazing Grace

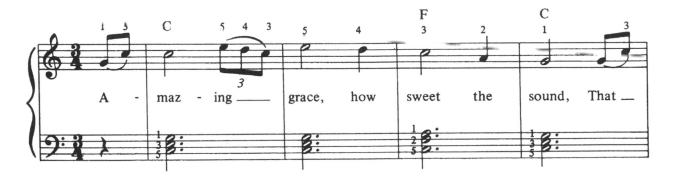

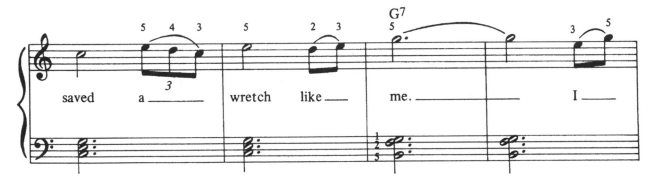

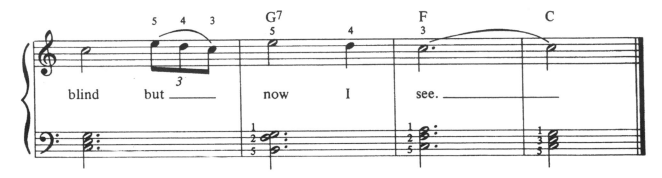

Sixteenth Notes

A *sixteenth note* is a short note that lasts for only a quarter of a beat. Here's how it fits in with the note values you have already learned.

As you know, eighth notes are counted with the word "and" between beats—as indicated by the ampersand sign (&) between numerals. The eighth notes in this example are counted "one-and-two-and-three-and-four-and." You'll need additional syllables to count the rhythm of sixteenth notes, which are counted "one-ee-and-ah, two-ee-and-ah, three-ee-and-ah, four-ee-and-ah." Count and clap this rhythm exercise.

Count and clap the opening phrases of "Listen to the Mockingbird." Note that the first sixteenth notes form a one-beat pickup (counted "four-ee-and-ah").

Sixteenth notes are often paired with dotted notes in song melodies. This pattern gives a characteristic lilting rhythm, as in the popular hit, "Wimoweh." This traditional South African Zulu song (retitled "The Lion Sleeps Tonight") became a number-one hit in 1961 for the Tokens, featuring Neil Sedaka. Robert John put it back on the charts for thirteen weeks in 1972.

Practice the melody with your right hand before adding the left hand.

Wimoweh

A - wim - o - weh, a - wim - o - weh, a - wim - o - weh, a - wim - o - weh, A -

wim - o - weh, a - wim - o - weh, a - wim - o - weh, a - wim - o - weh, A - wim - o - weh, a - wim - o - weh, a -

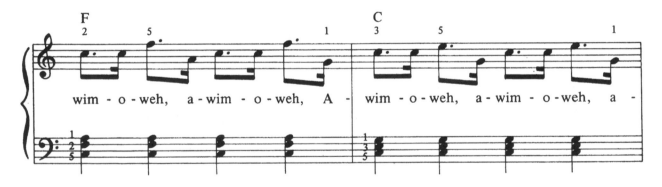

wim - o - weh, a - wim - o - weh, A - wim - o - weh, a - wim - o - weh, a -

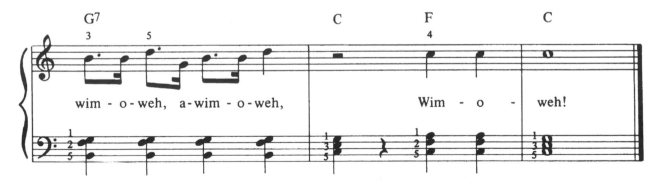

wim - o - weh, a - wim - o - weh, Wim - o - weh!

Sharps

So far, you've played several songs using the white keys of the piano keyboard: A, B, C, D, E, F, and G. As you may have already noticed, the black keys of the piano keyboard provide pitches in between these notes. These pitches are called *sharp notes* or *flat notes,* depending on their musical context. The names of these notes are formed by adding a sharp sign (♯) or flat sign (♭) after the note's letter name. These signs, as well as the notes themselves, are often called simply *sharps* and *flats.* The white-key notes are sometimes called *natural notes* (or *naturals*) to distinguish them from sharps or flats. Take a look at the sequence of the natural and sharp notes as they occur on the piano keyboard.

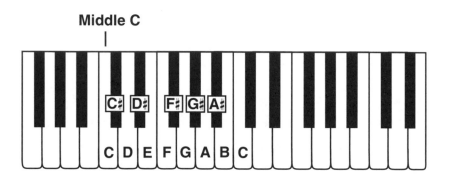

As you can see, each sharp key occurs just above the white key with the same letter name. Thus, the black note between the C and D notes is labeled C♯, the black note in between the D and E keys is D♯, and so on. Notice that no sharp occurs between the E and F keys—and none occurs between the B and C keys. This sequence of natural and sharp notes is known as a *chromatic scale.* Here's how the scale looks on the musical staff in both treble and bass clef.

Take the time to memorize the position and name of each of the sharp notes as they appear on the keyboard and staff. It's also important to remember that when a note appears with a sharp sign, all subsequent notes of that measure in that same position on the staff are also sharped, as indicated in this example. The barline cancels the sharp sign, so the final note is an A natural.

The following arrangement of the traditional Jewish folksong "Havah Nagilah" features an octave accompaniment. You'll have to stretch your left hand quite a bit to play this part. Practice this octave exercise with left pinky and thumb.

Several G♯ notes occur in the melody of "Havah Nagilah." Be aware that the second note in the third measure (corresponding with the syllable "-vah") is also a G♯ note. This G♯ note is not cancelled by the barline because it is tied over into the next measure. Practice the right hand of this traditional hora, then play it through twice with the indicated endings.

Havah Nagilah

Flats

In certain musical contexts, the black keys of the piano are viewed as flat notes rather than sharp notes. Take a look at the sequence of the natural and flat notes as they occur on the piano keyboard.

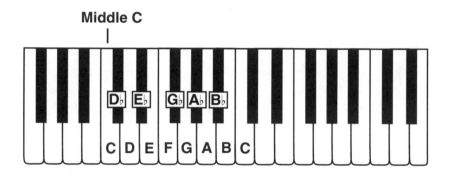

As you can see, flat notes occur one key lower than the white key of the same letter name on the piano keyboard. The flat sign appears after the letter name of the lowered white key to indicate the black-key name. Thus, the black-key note between the C and D notes is labeled D♭, the black-key note between the D and E keys is E♭, and so on. As with sharps, no flat occurs between the E and F keys, and none occurs between the B and C keys.

The descending version of the chromatic scale features natural notes and flats.

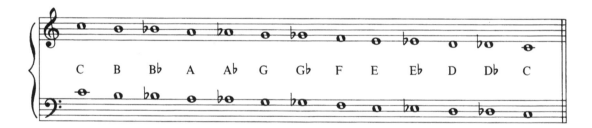

Take the time to memorize the name and position of each of these flats as they appear on the keyboard and staff. Also remember that if a note appears with a flat sign, all subsequent notes of that measure in the same position on the staff are also flatted, as indicated in this example. The barline cancels the flat sign, so the final note is an A natural.

"Rock Island Line" was a top-10 hit for Lonnie Donegan in 1956. The right-hand part of this memorable tune features an E♭ note. Practice the melody of "Rock Island Line," then add the chords with the left hand.

The Rock Island Line

Oh, the Rock Is - land Line, ___ it is a might-y good road, ___ Oh, the

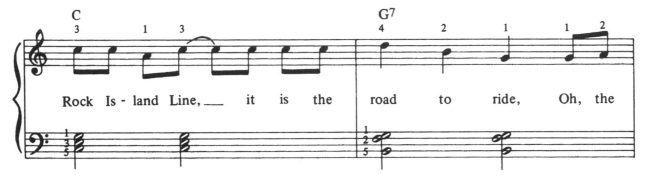

Rock Is - land Line, ___ it is the road to ride, Oh, the

Rock Is - land Line, ___ it is a might-y good road, ___ If you

want to ride it, got to ride it like you find it, Get your

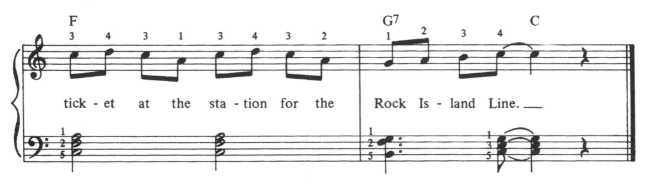

tick - et at the sta - tion for the Rock Is - land Line. ___

Naturals

Naturals are notes played on the white keys of the piano. A *natural sign* cancels a sharp or flat sign that has appeared with a note in the same position. Once a natural sign has been used, all other subsequent notes in the same position on the staff in that measure are affected by the natural sign.

As you might expect, a natural sign may be cancelled by a flat or sharp sign with a note of the same position in the same measure. Notice that the barline then cancels the sharp.

Some pieces contain both sharps and flats. Whether a note is flatted or sharped depends on its particular musical function in the piece. But, as a general rule, an *accidental* that leads up to a natural note is written as a sharp note—and an accidental that leads down to a natural note is written as a flat note. This rule is illustrated in this excerpt from "My Melancholy Baby."

With your right hand, play the melody of "The Old Grey Mare," which features naturals and sharps. Once you are familiar with the melody, add the chords with your left hand.

The Old Grey Mare

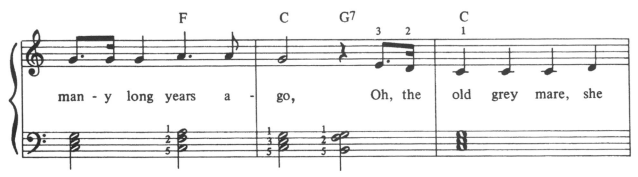

The C7 Chord

The C7 chord is simply a C major chord with an added B♭ note—the flatted seventh degree of the C major scale. This chord is also called the I7 chord in the key of C major.

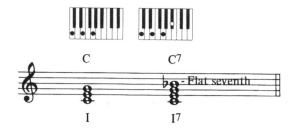

Here are the C, G7, C7, and F chords notated in bass clef for the left hand. Notice that the G note is not included in the C7 chord, so it can be played using three fingers. Practice playing these chords in sequence.

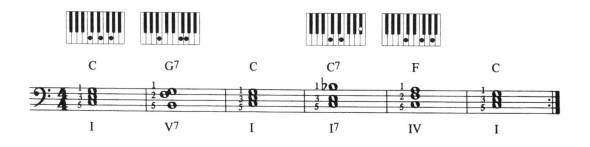

Once you are familiar with the chord exercise, practice the left hand of the favorite college song, "Goodnight Ladies." Then add the melody part with the right hand. Once you've played "Goodnight Ladies" (which contains the C7 and G7 chords), turn to the "Table of Chords" in the back of the book to practice all the other seventh chords (D7, E7, F7, A7, and so on).

Goodnight Ladies

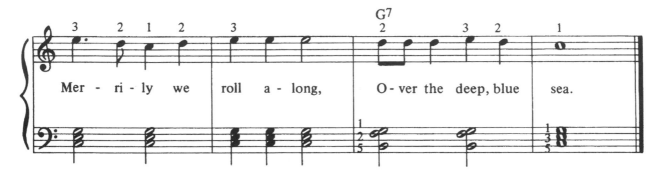

Minor Chords

So far, you've learned the important major chords in the key of C. The triads that occur on the second and sixth degree of the scale in all keys are important minor chords. These are known as IIm and VIm, respectively, and correspond to the Dm and Am chords in the key of C.

A listing of all major and minor chords for all keys is included in a comprehensive "Table of Chords" at the end of this book. Take the time to learn and practice all of these chords. As you practice these chords, you'll soon see that a minor chord is simply formed by altering one note of the corresponding major chord—that is, the third of the major chord is lowered by one half step. Compare the D major and D minor chords.

D Major   D Minor

Minor chords often add a certain sad or introspective quality to a piece—and can add the perfect touch to a love ballad or any song that creates a personal portrait or calls up visions of the past. This arrangement of "Molly Malone" (also known as "Cockles and Mussels") features the Dm, C, Am, F, G, and G7 chords (the IIm, I, IV, V, and V7 chords in the key of C). Note that the Dm chord only appears in the intro section of the piece—while the Am chord is included in this recurring chord pattern: C, Am F, G. Practice this chord exercise.

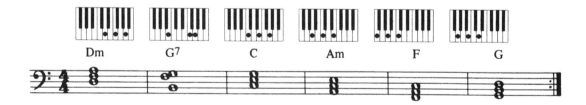

Now practice the left hand of the ballad "Molly Malone," which features broken chords. Once you are familiar with the harmony, add the melody with the right hand. Finger numbering in the melody will guide you to the correct hand positions. You'll see that it's sometimes necessary to switch fingers when playing repeated notes, as in measures 9 and 10. Notice how the minor chords add to the sentimental quality of this traditional favorite.

Molly Malone

Introduction

Dynamics

The pattern of volume in a composition or performance is called its *dynamics*. Take the time to memorize these common markings and their corresponding meanings in Italian and English.

pp = **Pianissimo** = Very soft

p = **Piano** = Soft

mp = **Mezzo piano** = Moderately soft

mf = **Mezzo forte** = Moderately loud

f = **Forte** = Loud

ff = **Fortissimo** = Very loud

A gradual increase in volume is called *crescendo*. Begin softly and gradually get louder as you play the first exercise below.

A decrease in volume is called a *diminuendo*. Begin loudly and gradually get softer as you play the second exercise.

Crescendo **Diminuendo**

Review the dynamic markings in "Hail! Hail! the Gang's All Here," then practice this rousing piece with both hands. If you play an electronic keyboard or synthesizer that isn't touch sensitive, you'll need to adjust the master volume with a volume pedal or hand control to vary the dynamics in a piece.

Hail! Hail! the Gang's All Here

Tempo

Composers and arrangers use Italian or English terms to indicate how fast a piece should be played. These *tempo markings* usually appear at the beginning of a piece or section. Here are some of the more common Italian tempo markings and their English equivalents.

Lento (or **Largo**) = Very slow

Adagio = Slow

Andante = Walking pace

Moderato = Medium

Allegretto = Medium fast

Allegro = Fast

Presto = Very fast

Prestissimo = As fast as possible

Variations in tempo within a piece are often used to provide contrast in music, particularly in longer works.

Sometimes a composer or arranger wishes to indicate that the regular beat or tempo of a piece should hold or pause for a moment on a specific note or rest. This hold or pause is indicated with a *fermata* (⌢).

Certain terms call for changing of the tempo. The term *ritardando* (often abbreviated as *ritard.* or *rit.*) indicates that the tempo should slow down.

Accelerando calls for a quickening of the tempo.

The term *a tempo* (pronounced "ah tempo") tells the musician to return to the normal speed of the piece.

You will soon get a chance to practice tempo changes when you play "Danny Boy." First practice this chord exercise with your left hand.

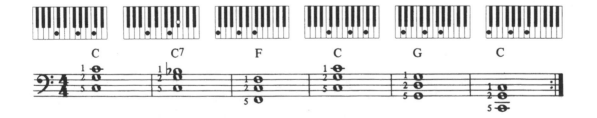

Now take a minute to review the music for "Danny Boy." This traditional Irish ballad has been recorded by a range of different artists—from Bing Crosby to Conway Twitty.

First play the melody of "Danny Boy" with your right hand. Note the fingering crosses in measures 3, 11, 28, and 30. Once you are familiar with the melody, play the piece with both hands. In measure 6, both thumbs play the melody note—Middle C. Notice the overall tempo is *adagio* (slow)—and that fermatas and ritandandos add to the song's emotional power.

Danny Boy

The Key of C Major

The number of sharps or flats that occur regularly in a piece of music determines the key. These symbols are written in a key signature at the beginning of each staff. Many of the musical examples in the book so far have been written in the key of C major, which has no sharps or flats.

Composers and arrangers write music in different keys to bring out the best in a particular composition or musical instrument. Once you understand the construction of the scale in the key of C major, you'll be able to build the scale and key signature for every other major key.

The shortest distance between two notes is called a *half step*. A *whole step* is the equivalent of two half steps. Let's examine the pattern of whole steps and half steps in the C major scale. Take the time to memorize this pattern, which is the blueprint for all other major scales.

Remember, you should cross your thumb under your third finger going up the scale. When you come down the scale, cross your third finger over your thumb. Practice the scale exercise above until you can play it smoothly and evenly.

Now play "Michael, Row the Boat Ashore," which was a number one chart hit for the Highwaymen in 1961. This arrangement features the C, F, and G7 chords (the familiar I, IV, and V7 chords in the key of C).

Michael, Row the Boat Ashore

The Key of G Major

Once you are familiar with the step pattern of the C major scale, take a look at the G major scale. This new scale requires an F♯ note in order to follow the major scale pattern. Practice this scale using the indicated fingering.

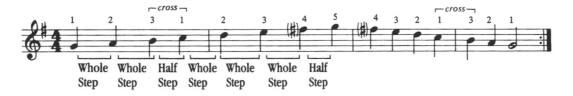

Since the F♯ note is a regular feature in the key of G major, it is shown in the key signature after the clef on every staff of the piece. This indicates that all F notes in the piece will be sharped unless otherwise marked.

Here are G, C, and D7 chords (the I, IV, and V7 chords in the key of G, respectively). The D7 chord is a new one for you—and requires an F♯ note. Play each of these chords in sequence with the left hand.

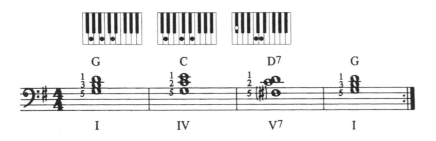

Now play "Michael, Row the Boat Ashore" in the key of G

Michael, Row the Boat Ashore (Key of G Major)

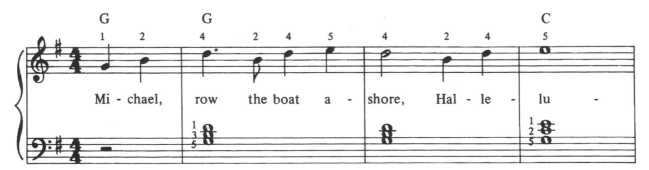

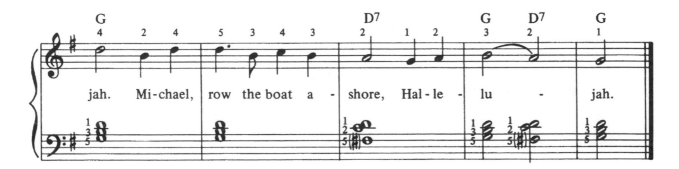

The Keys of D and A Major

Once you know the step-by-step pattern that forms all major scales, it's easy to play in any major key. In this and the next sections, you'll explore major keys that are common in piano music—and easy to play. You'll get a chance to play several more songs in these keys later on in the book.

Practice each of these major scales and chord patterns using the indicated fingering. Accidentals are provided in parentheses to remind you of the flats or sharps that appear in the key signature.

D Major Scale

Basic Chords in D Major

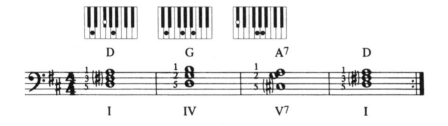

A Major Scale

Basic Chords in A Major

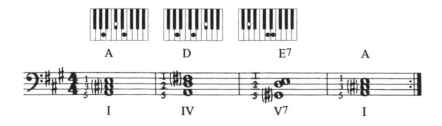

Now play "Michael, Row the Boat Ashore" in the keys of D Major and A Major.

Michael, Row the Boat Ashore (Key of D Major)

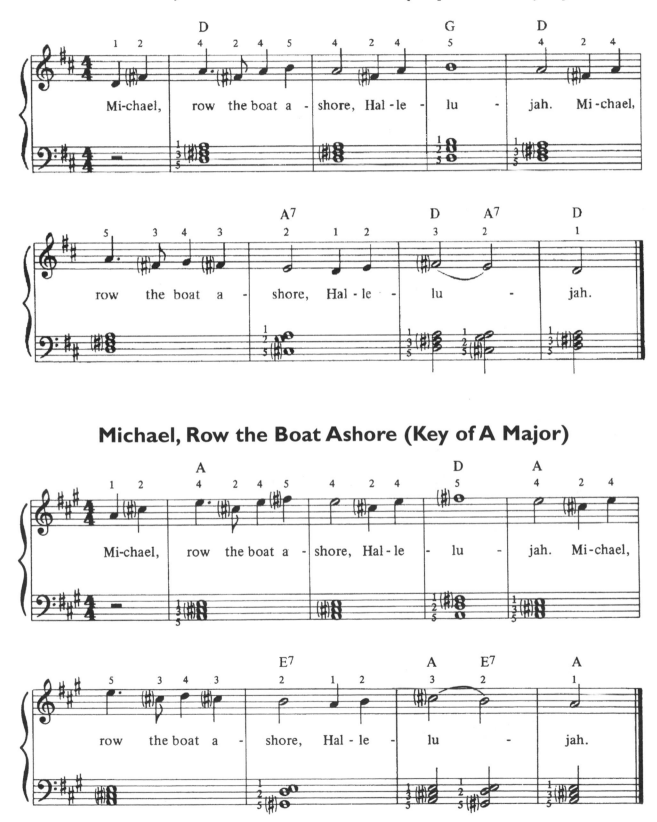

Michael, Row the Boat Ashore (Key of A Major)

The Keys of F and B♭ Major

Now let's focus on the key signatures that contain flats. Here's the F major scale, which features one flat, followed by the B♭ major scale, with two flats. Practice each of these scales and basic chord patterns using the indicated fingering.

F Major Scale

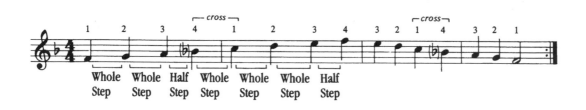

Basic Chords in F Major

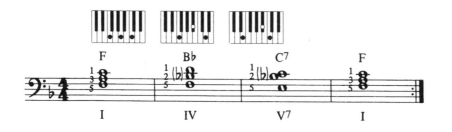

B♭ Major Scale

Basic Chords in B♭ Major

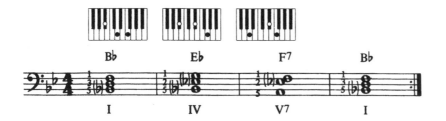

Michael, Row the Boat Ashore (Key of F Major)

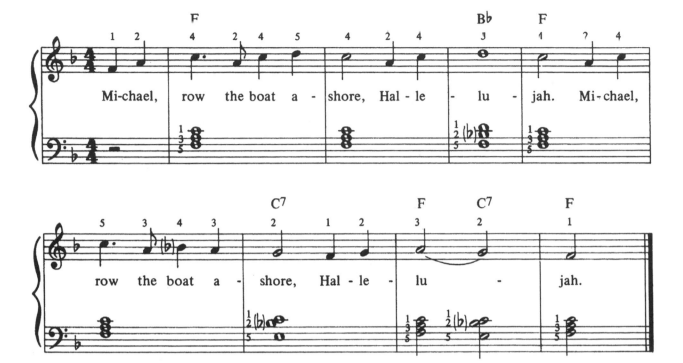

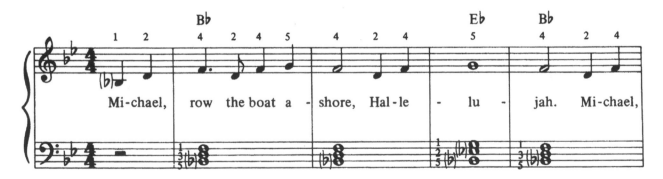

Michael, Row the Boat Ashore (Key of B♭ Major)

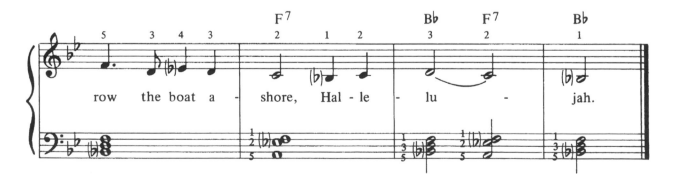

Minor Keys

As you know, music may be written in different keys to accommodate the ranges of particular voices or instruments. Another reason for writing a piece in a particular key is to lend a special tonal color, or tonality, to a piece. Many of the musical excerpts you have studied in this book so far have been written in a major key, and therefore have major tonalities. Sometimes a composer chooses to use a minor key to lend a dark, introspective, or sad quality to a piece. A minor key is formed by lowering certain notes of the corresonding major scale (usually the third, sixth, and seventh scale degrees).

You really don't need to know all the technical rules regarding minor keys in order to play in them. Just pay attention to the flats (or sharps) indicated in the key signature when you play the song—just as you would when playing in a major key.

In the earlier section, "Minor Chords," you learned that a minor triad is formed by lowering the third of the corresponding major chord. The folk favorite "The Erie Canal" is written here in the key of C minor—with three flats in the key signature (Bb, Eb, and Ab). In this song, the Bb note is always made a natural by an accidental.

The left-hand part of "The Erie Canal" features the C minor, F minor, and G7 chords (the I minor, IV minor, and V7 chords). Practice these three chords in sequence with the left hand. Be sure to include the Eb note and Ab note, as indicated by accidentals in parentheses, and to use B natural instead of Bb.

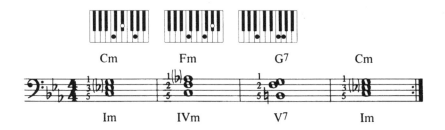

This arrangement of "The Erie Canal" features a lowered third (the Eb note) and lowered sixth (the Ab note). Accidentals are provided in parentheses in the first two measures only. After that, you'll have to watch out for these flat notes on your own. Practice the melody with your right hand until you can play it with ease. Then play the song using both hands. Remember to slow down when you reach the *ritard.* at the end of the piece.

The Erie Canal

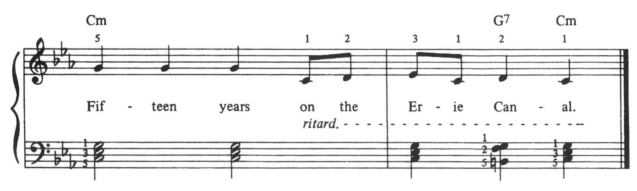

Blues

The blues was born in the American South. It evolved from the work songs written by African-American slaves before the Civil War—and was deeply influenced by African rhythms and tonality. The blues is known for its power to evoke the listener's emotions. The blues lyric often tells a personal story of troubles and longing. The plaintive melody and harmony of the blues, coupled with its strong and simple rhythm, make it a universally appealing musical form.

Most blues melodies and solos are based on the pentatonic blues scale. This scale has only five notes per octave (instead of seven, as found in the major and minor scales). Notice the *blue notes* are lowered by one half-step with flats. These notes correspond to the flatted third and seventh degrees of the major scale which give the blues its dark and mournful sound.

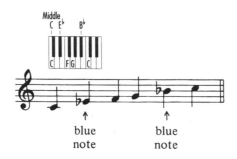

Good Morning Blues

Many traditional blues songs and modern blues-rock tunes are written in twelve-bar blues form—with twelve bars (or measures) in each complete verse of the song. "Good Morning Blues" is a classic twelve-bar blues song that has been recorded by many of the great blues masters. This tune features the standard blues chords—I7, IV7, and V7. In the key of C, these chords are C7, F7, and G7. Practice the following exercise with your left hand.

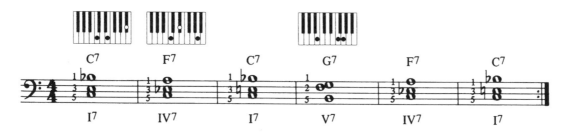

Blues pianists know that a hard-driving sense of rhythm is what makes a great blues performance. Count aloud as you play this characteristic rhythm with the left hand. Notice that the second chord in measures three and four jumps in a little early to add some excitement to the blues beat. This important rhythm technique, called *syncopation,* is a trademark of the blues—and an integral feature of jazz as well.

Now play the melody to "Good Morning Blues" with your right hand. In this arrangement, the last note of the each melody phrase jumps in a little early to create a bluesy syncopation.

Once you are familiar with the melody, play this classic song using both hands.

Good Morning Blues

Frankie and Johnny

"Frankie and Johnny" is perhaps the most famous blues of all time. This stark take of love and murder was recorded by many great blues artists—and was a signature tune for Mae West. As a testament to this song's versatility, rhythm & blues singer/songwriter Brook Benton put it on the charts for four weeks in 1961 and soul singer Sam Cooke put it back on the charts for seven weeks in 1963. Elvis Presley made it a hit once again for five weeks in 1966.

Practice this chord pattern with your left hand.

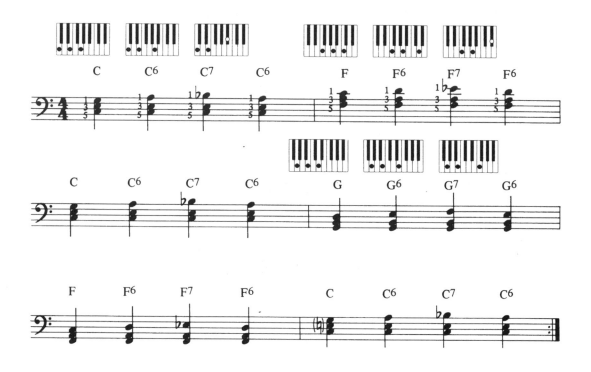

Now play this jazzy chord—the C13♯11—using both hands.

Practice the melody part of "Frankie and Johnny" with your right hand, then play the song with both hands together. Be sure to roll the final C13#11 chord from the bottom up, as indicated by the wavy line.

Frankie and Johnny

Rock

Rock and roll emerged in the 1950s as "rockabilly" music—a blending of hillbilly-style country music and the driving beat of Black rhythm & blues. Rock's pioneers include Bill Haley, Carl Perkins, Chuck Berry, Elvis Presley, Jerry Lee Lewis, and Little Richard. In the 1960s, the popularity of rock music was brought to a new peak with the advent of British rock groups, beginning with the Beatles, the Who, and the Rolling Stones. Today, rock and roll is the predominant musical style on the pop charts. In this section, you'll get to play two classic rock hits.

C.C. Rider

"C.C. Rider" is an all-time favorite blues-rock song that has been performed by a range of artists. Ma Rainey brought this tune to position fourteen on the charts in 1925. In 1957, rhythm and blues singer Chuck Willis had a career-making hit with this song—and inspired the dance craze called "The Stroll." In 1963, rhythm and blues singer LaVern Baker recorded her hit version of this tune (entitled "See See Rider"). The magic had not worn off this terrific rhythm number—for Eric Burdon & the Animals made "See See Rider" a hit once again for seven weeks in 1966.

Before you try "C.C. Rider," practice this chord exercise with your right hand. Once you have mastered this exercise, practice the left-hand part of "C.C. Rider" until you can play it with confidence at a steady rock beat. Then play the tune using both hands together.

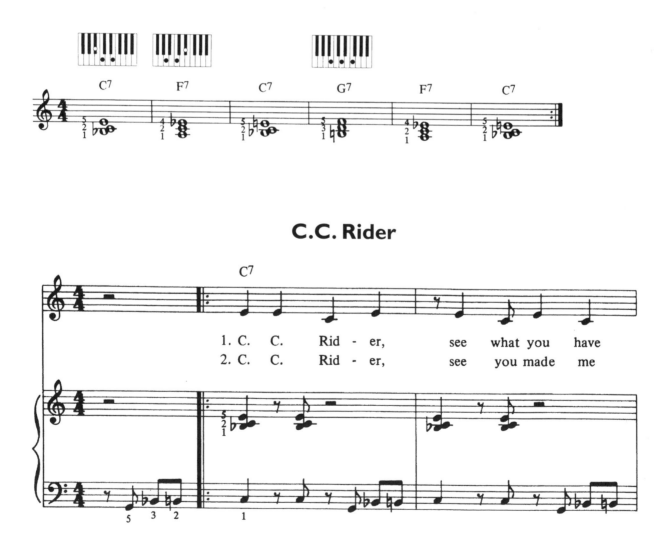

La Bamba

Latin rock and roll star Ritchie Valens made a hit with "La Bamba" in 1959. The movie based on his life, *La Bamba,* was released in 1987—with music by the Latin-American rock quintet Los Lobos.

Practice the left- and right-hand parts separately before you play this one—then play it with both hands together. Once you can play "La Bamba" at a moderate tempo with ease, work to play the tune at a fast and steady beat. Place some added stress on the first and third beats of every measure, and you'll bring out the Latin flavor of this terrific dance tune.

La Bamba

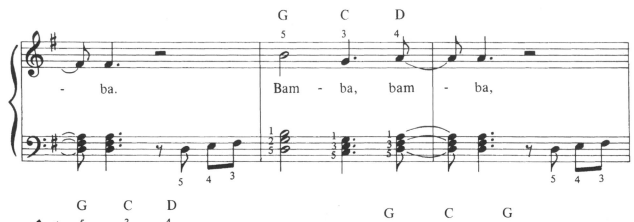

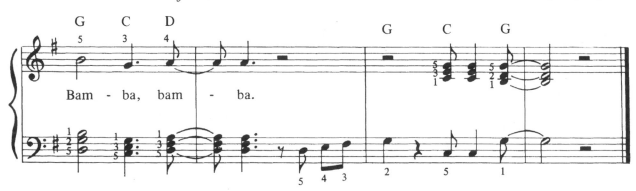

Pop

The term *pop music* refers to any music that features contemporary lyrics, standard chord patterns, bright vocals, and electronic instrumentation. Pop music differs from rock and roll in that it does not traditionally feature a jarring beat, pitch-bending, or raw vocals and instrumentals.

Contemporary pop and rock music developed during the 1950s. Early pop music took several forms: there were "doo-wop" groups (like the Marcels and the Five Satins); close-harmony vocal ensembles (like the Supremes and Shirelles); and groups doing "surf" music (notably, the Beach Boys and Jan and Dean).

Throughout the sixties and seventies, pop was more and more influenced by rock music—and today, many pop chart hits are actually rock, pop-rock, or "soft" rock music. Today's pop-rock hits are usually dance tunes, and feature strong and evocative rhythms. In this section, you'll focus on hits of the classic pop period as you play the music of Cat Stevens, Elvis Presley, and the Beach Boys.

Morning Has Broken

"Morning Has Broken" is a traditional hymn that captured the attention of singer/songwriter Cat Stevens. In 1972, his hit recording of this beautiful tune stayed on the charts for eleven weeks, peaking at position six. This arrangement of "Morning Has Broken" features chords played one note at a time (called *arpeggios)* in the left hand, and sounds best when played smoothly and evenly.

First practice the chords.

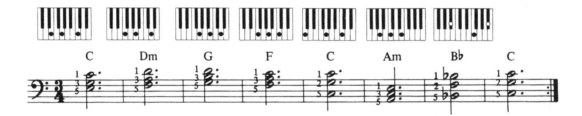

The dynamic markings in "Morning Has Broken" will help bring out the personality in your performance. The marking *p-mf* indicates that the first verse should be played softly and the second verse medium-loud. For this song, you may wish to lift and depress your sustain pedal at the beginning of each measure. This is the pedal of the far right of a standard piano. If you are using an electric piano or synthesizer, you may eventually want to add a sustain pedal to your instrument if you don't already have one.

Morning Has Broken

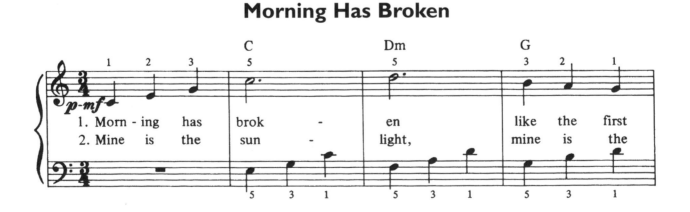

Sloop John B.

Originally a West Indian folk song, "Sloop *John B.*" became a favorite of the Beach Boys in 1966.
Practice this chord exercise, which includes the F, B♭, C7, C9, and B♭m chords.

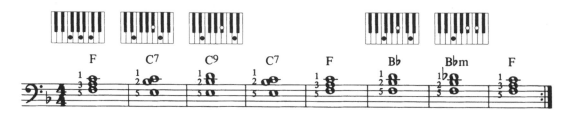

Once you become familiar with the melody, play "Sloop *John B.*" at a slow to moderate tempo
with both hands.

Sloop John B.

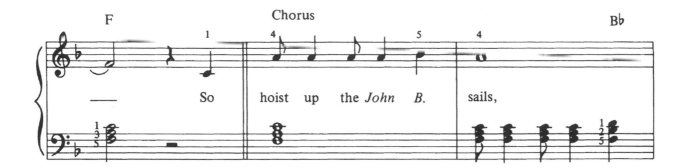

So hoist up the *John B.* sails,

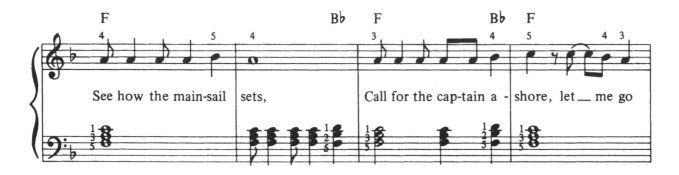

See how the main-sail sets, Call for the cap-tain a - shore, let _ me go

home. _____ Let _ me go home,

I want _ to go home, I feel so break up,

I want _ to go home. _____

Aura Lee (Love Me Tender)

"Aura Lee," composed by George R. Poulton, has long been considered one of America's most popular love melodies. It enjoyed a smash revival in 1956 when Elvis Presley recorded it as "Love Me Tender." This chart-busting hit was the title song for Elvis's first movie, remaining in the number one position on the charts for five weeks. It was back on the charts when Richard Chamberlain recorded it in 1962—and Percy Sledge, in 1967.

Elvis's hit tune makes a terrific slow pop-rock piano solo. Before you play the arrangement, practice this exercise to get familiar with the chord sequence that provides the harmony in the left-hand part. Several chords are used in this exercise—including G, Am, D, D7, G+, C, and Cm. Note that the G+ chord is a new chord form called *G augmented*. Some of the chord inversions in this exercise require a full octave stretch of the left hand. Because two of the chords in this exercise are quite high on the bass staff, they are written in treble clef. This is a challenging chord exercise that may require a little extra practice—but the results in "Aura Lee" are well worth it.

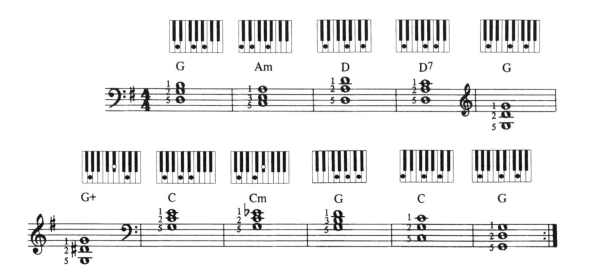

Once you are familiar with the chord exercise, practice the left-hand part of the arrangement, which features an interesting arpeggio pattern. There are two basic arpeggio fingerings: 5-1-2-1 and 5-2-1-2,.

Practice the left-hand part slowly and evenly until you can play each pattern smoothly in tempo. After you've mastered it, play this beautiful love song with both hands together.

Aura Lee (Love Me Tender)

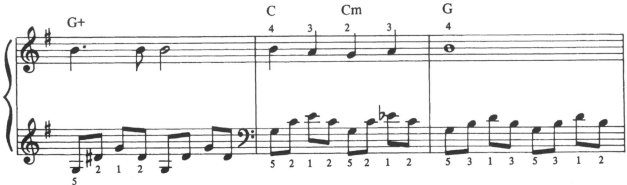

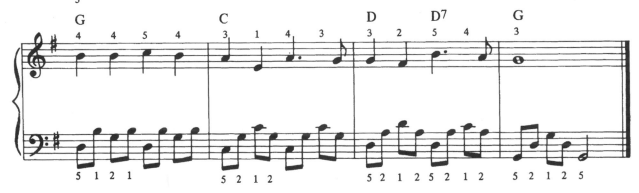

Ragtime

Like the blues, ragtime emerged from traditional African-American folk music of the nineteenth century. Ragtime's inventors are thought to have been travelling minstrels who combined elements of Euro-American folk dance and fiddle music with syncopated African rhythms to create a new distinctive musical genre. Ragtime music is characterized by a syncopated melody played with a steady, march-like harmony part.

The Entertainer

Ragtime has enjoyed lasting fame in the music of Scott Joplin—who was the first ragtime composer to put his music on paper. "The Entertainer" was revived in the movie *The Sting,* and made Scott Joplin's name a household word in the 1970s and beyond.

Practice this chord exercise with your left hand.

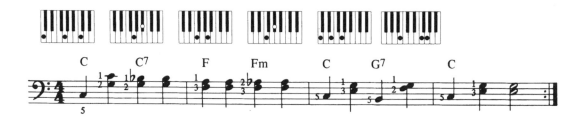

Now play "The Entertainer" at a moderately slow tempo.

The Entertainer

Jazz

Jazz first became popular in the New Orleans area at the turn of the century. This early jazz is often termed New Orleans jazz. Most historians agree that jazz is a direct descendant of ragtime and the blues. Like the blues, once jazz spread to other urban centers around the country, it took on new forms. Dixieland and Harlem style jazz added some sophistication to the basic sound—and explored the potential of different instruments in the jazz band.

Like its predecessors ragtime and blues, jazz music explored suggestive new rhythms that raised some eyebrows among the conservative set, and inspired many new dance crazes among the more adventurous. In the 1920s, jazz entered the mainstream of popular song and made its debut on the Broadway stage. Since jazz is largely an instrumental form, musicians found that many older songs could be "jazzed up" to enjoy successful revivals. If a song was played enough by jazz musicians, it became known as a jazz standard.

Through the years, jazz claimed many popular songs, folk tunes, and blues songs for its own. Standards include traditional songs like "A-Tisket A-Tasket" and "Frankie and Johnny," as well as commercial hits like "Tea for Two" and "Alexander's Ragtime Band." In fact, most of the songs written by jazz-influenced composers such as Irving Berlin, George Gershwin, and Jerome Kern were reinterpreted by jazz musicians as standard pieces in their repertoire.

A-Tisket A-Tasket

Ella Fitzgerald is perhaps the greatest jazz singer of all time. After winning the Harlem Amateur Hour in 1934, she created a popular sensation with her jazzy rendition of "A-Tisket A-Tasket."

The secret to a successful jazz performance is a rhythmic technique called *syncopation*. Syncopated rhythms focus stress on beats that are not normally stressed in other forms of music. For example, classical, rock, and pop compositions in $\frac{4}{4}$ time stress the first and third beats of each measure, as in the first line of "A-Tisket A-Tasket," shown below.

A tis - ket, a tas - ket, a green and yel - low bas - ket;

However, a jazz composition in $\frac{4}{4}$ time often features syncopated notes and words just before or after the stressed beats of the music—on the *offbeats* or *upbeats* of the rhythm. Ella Fitzgerald used this phrasing to achieve a swingy feel in this number, as illustrated on the following page. Before you play "A-Tisket A-Tasket," practice the chord exercise below, which features the Cmaj7, C6, Dm7, and G7 chords.

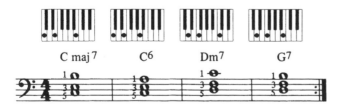

Once you become familiar with the exercise, practice the right-hand part of "A-Tisket A Tasket." Then play the song using both hands.

A-Tisket A-Tasket

Classical

Technically speaking, *classical music* is any serious music composed between 1750 and 1820. This term is also commonly applied to music of a serious nature composed in any period—from the late Renaissance to the present. Throughout the centuries, classical composers have concentrated on the development of musical structure and form in their work. With the invention of new musical instruments and playing techniques, each generation of classical composers has worked to explore the limits of solo, ensemble, and orchestral performance.

Bridal Chorus

Get ready to play Wagner's famous "Bridal Chorus" from the opera *Lohengrin*. Like any march in ²⁄₄ time, this piece should be played with a steady and confident beat—with a bit of extra stress on notes that occur on the first beat of each measure.

Bridal Chorus

Table of Notes

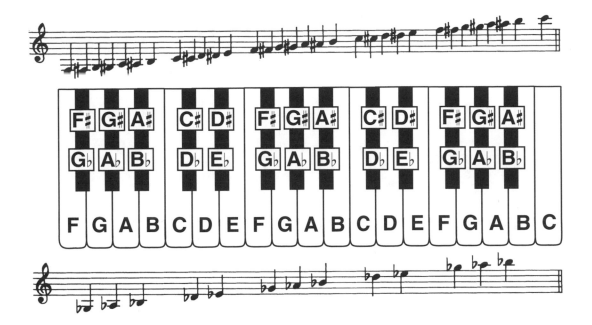

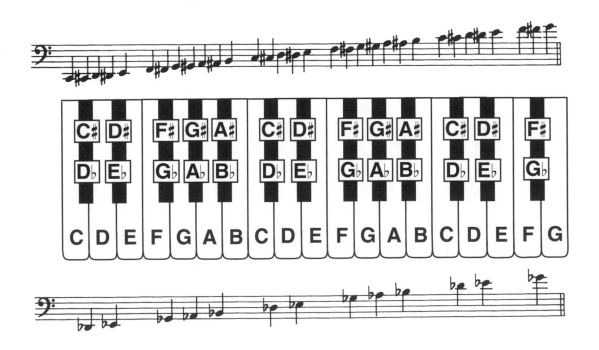

Table of Chords